Hello!
I am a spider.

Most spiders have 8 eyes.

But some have just 6, 4 or even zero eyes.

Spiders come in a variety of shapes, sizes, colors and danger levels

There are over 48,000 different species of spiders around the world.

Many spiders are "nocturnal". That means they are most active during the night.

Some male spiders perform special dances to attract female spiders.

I like to boogey.

Not all spiders spin webs.

Some spiders hunt by actively chasing and capturing their prey.

Some spiders can jump up to 50 times their body length to catch prey or escape from danger.

How high can you jump?

The largest spider in the world is the "Goliath Birdeater".

I have a leg span of up to 11 inches (28 cm).

Many spiders are tiny and harmless to humans.

I couldn't hurt a fly.

They're too big.

Spiders have an "exoskeleton".

I don't have bones in my body.

An exoskeleton is like a hard outer shell of the body.

My exoskeleton protects and supports me.

A spider's muscles are attached to their exoskeleton.

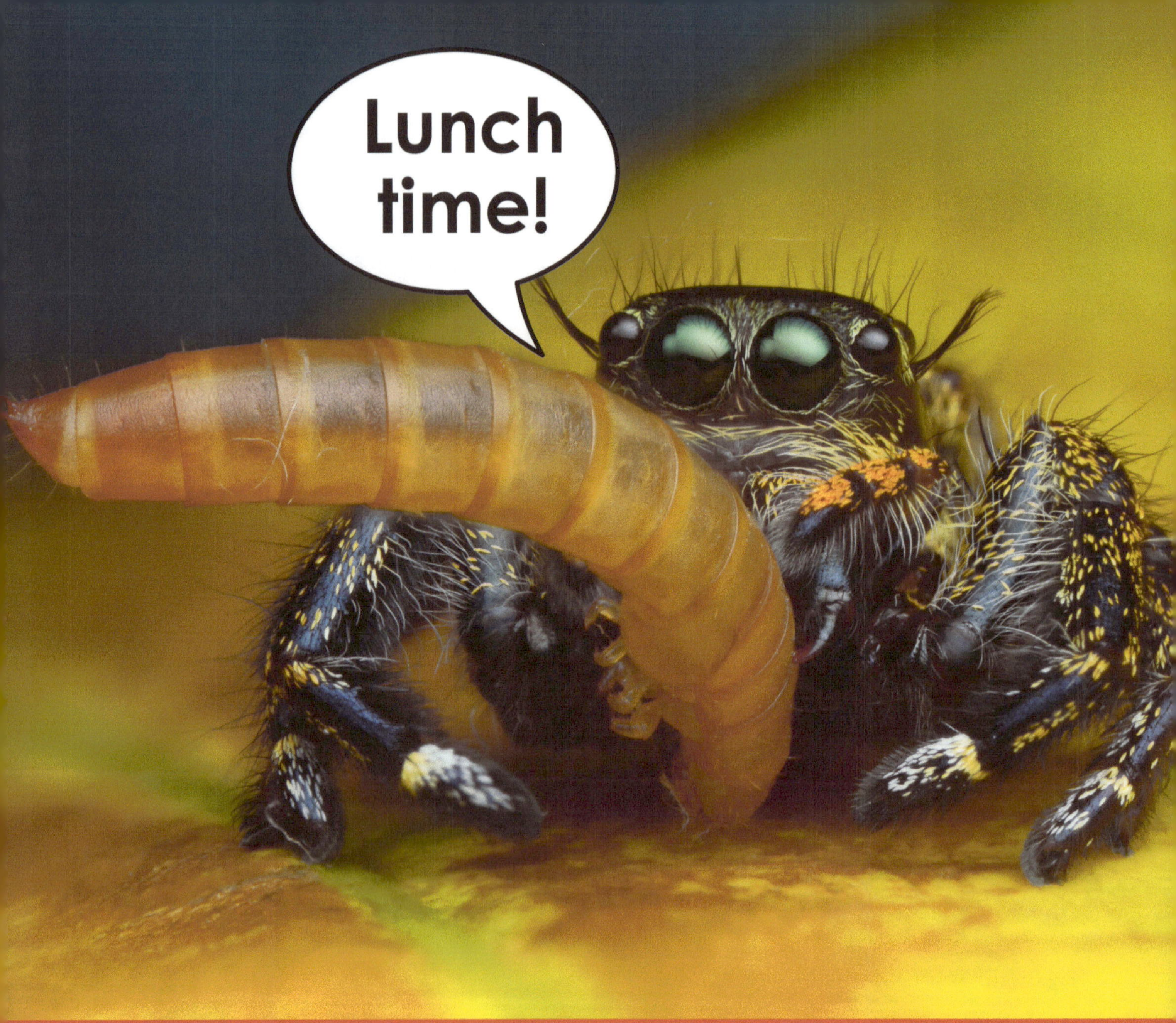

Spiders are “carnivores”. That means they eat other animals.

Some spiders wrap their prey in silk before eating.

I'll take this *to go*.

Spiders make silk with special glands in their abdomen.

It comes out the back.

The silk that spiders use to make webs is stronger than steel.

Every spider web has a unique design.

Spiders have tiny hairs on their legs that can feel vibrations in the web.

I can *feel* when prey is caught or when another spider is nearby.

Some spiders eat their own web and recycle the silk to make a new one.

Spiders use their webs for various purposes, such as catching food, creating a safe place to hide, or even as a home for resting.

Home sweet home.

Some spiders can spin a complete web in just a few hours.

Being a spider is a lot of work.

Some spiders take down their webs during the day to avoid predators and rebuild them at night.

Spider babies start their lives as eggs inside a strong silk sac.

This will be a safe place to start a family.

Baby spiders are called "spiderlings".

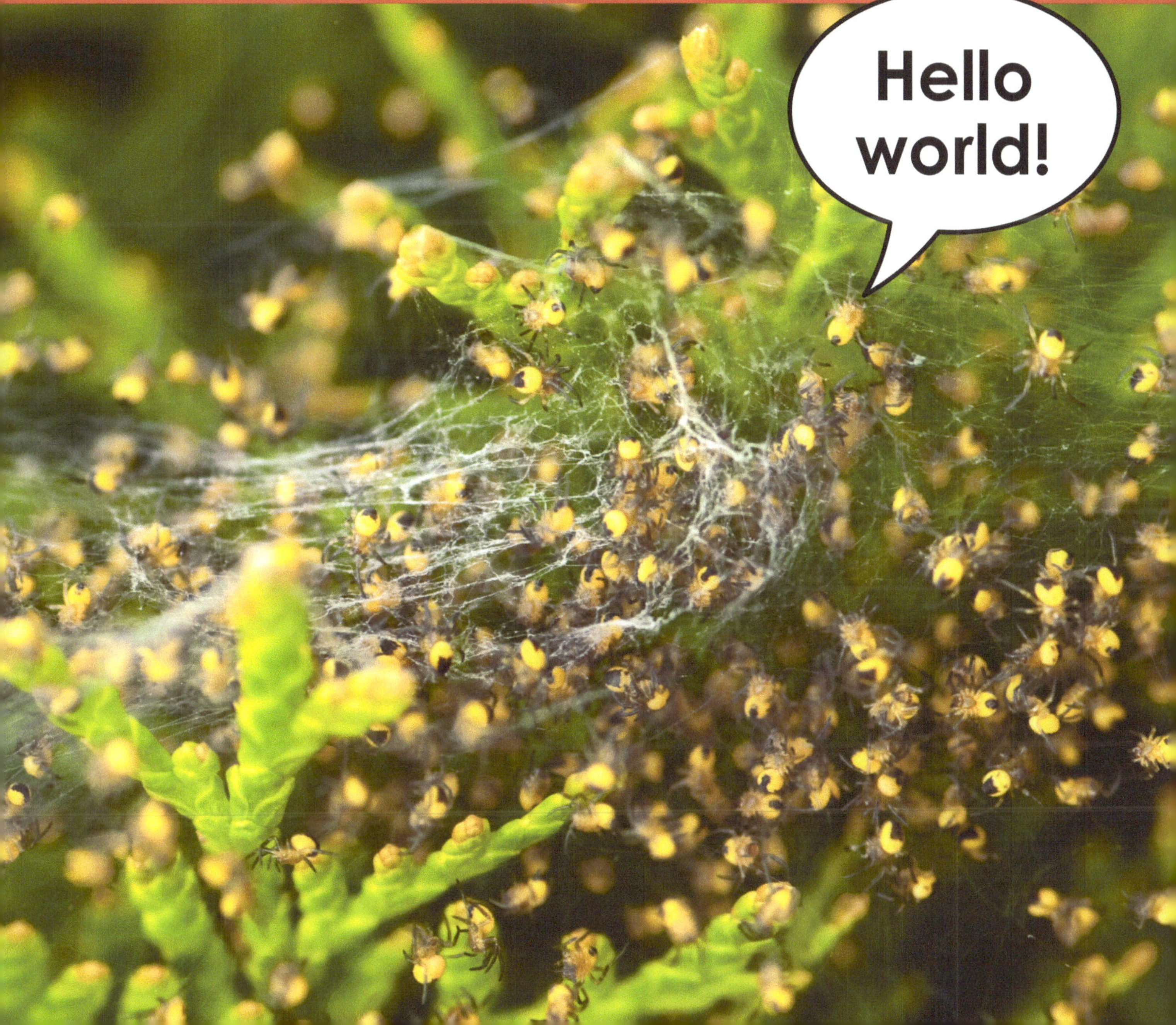

Some spiderling species don't rely on their mothers for food.

Some spider mothers carry around their spiderlings for protection and travel.

Spiders inject venom through their fangs for protection or to catch prey.

Don't mess with me.

The venom that spiders use to catch insects is __usually__ not harmful to humans.

But sometimes it's deadly.

Want more?

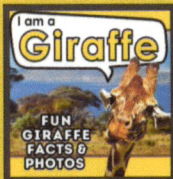      

 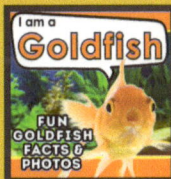     

  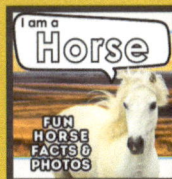    

   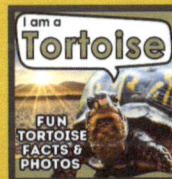  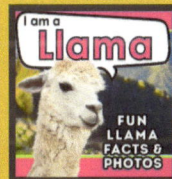 

  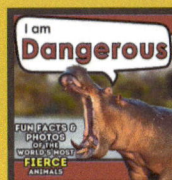   ... and more

COLLECT THEM ALL!

ActiveBrainsBooks.com

Hello parents!

scan here

Visit us to find out about new releases and **FREE** offers. We'll let you know when we have a new release coming out and how you can get it for FREE.

And you can cast your vote for what book we make next!

or visit here

ActiveBrainsBooks.com

scan here

Let us know what you think. As an independent publisher, your honest reviews mean a lot to us and our business. We'd love to hear from you!

or visit here

amazon.com/review/create-review/

FOLLOW US on Amazon.

amazon.com/author/activebrainsbooks

ActiveBrainsBooks.com

ACTIVE
BRAINS

www.ingramcontent.com/pod-product-compliance
Lightning Source LLC
Chambersburg PA
CBHW060844270326
41933CB00003B/193